ONE PLANET

NATURAL RESOURCES

Annabel Griffin

First published by Hungry Tomato Ltd in 2021
F1, Old Bakery Studios, Blewetts Wharf,
Malpas Road, Truro, Cornwall, TR1 1QH, UK.

www.hungrytomato.com

ISBN 978 1 914087 02 8

A CIP catalogue record for this book is available from
the British Library

Manufactured in the USA

Picture credits

(t=top; b=bottom; c=center; l=left; r=right;
bg=background)

Corbis 13tr, 16t. Drakewell Museum, Pennsylvania
Historical & Museum Commission 10bl. FLPA
7br (before), 23br, 24tl, 24cl, 28bl. NaturePL
24bl. Photodisc (Corbis) 9tl, 9tr. Shutterstock: 4l;
13b; 17br; 18bl; 26cl; Alena Ozerova 26b;arosoft
17cr; Arturo Limon 17bl (copper);beersonic 1bg;
BGSmith 4bg; Cheryl Casey 22tl; Christina
Tisi-Kramer 5cr; David G Hayes 7cr; Dudarev
Mikhail 18bg; E. Petersen 28bg; egd 21tr; Elena
Elisseeva 27cl; Francois BOIZOT 21bl; Galyna
Andrushko 6bg; Gordon Ball LRPS 25cr; Holger
Wulschlaeger 15tr; Igor Grochev 17c (amethyst);
IRC 10bg; Ivonne Wierink 28cl; ixpert 4b; Jacobs
photography 2bg; Keith McIntyre 17bc (mica);
Kitnha 7br (after); lostbear 9cl; Mats 9c; Media
Home 21br; Mikhail Olykainen 18tl; New Africa
9bc, 12bg; Norman Chan 16cl; Otmar Smit 27bl;
Pavol Kmeto 18cl; Prostock-studio 12bl; Rich Carey
23tr; Sascha Burkard 25br; sharon kingston 5tr;
sirtravelalot 6cl; Stock-Asso 5br; Studio Araminta
17tr; sunsetman 29tl; Szymon Apanowicz 21tl;
TierneyMJ 14-15c; Tina Rencelj 7bl; Vasily Smirnov
18bc; VectorMine 11tr, 11cr, 11br; Volodymyr
TVERDOKHLIB 24bg. Superstock: 8t, 9bl, 10l,
15br, 20bg, 21cl, 22b.

Every effort has been made to trace the copyright
holders, and we apologize in advance for any
unintentional omissions. We would be pleased to insert
the appropriate acknowledgments in any subsequent
edition of this publication.

CONTENTS

1. EARTH'S NATURAL RESOURCES

Look around you. Everything in your daily life – your toothbrush, the food for your lunch, the clothes you wear, the heat in your home – can be traced back to Earth's natural resources. Natural resources are the materials and sources of energy that come from our planet.

Gifts That Keep on Giving

As their name tells us, Earth's resources all come from nature. They include water, plant and animal life, coal, oil, minerals, and energy from wind and the Sun. People all over the world depend on Earth's natural resources for their survival. We also depend on them to provide everything that helps make our lives more comfortable, interesting, and enjoyable. But it is up to us to take care of these resources. We need to be sure that they will be around for many generations.

Like water and the Sun, wind is a renewable resource and can be used to generate electricity.

About 70% of Earth's surface is made up of water.

The Blue Planet

All the water on Earth today has been here since our planet was formed billions of years ago! And, as far as anyone knows, it is all the water that will ever be on Earth. About 97 percent of Earth's water is salt water in the oceans. Less than 3 percent is fresh water. Much of Earth's fresh water is frozen in ice. It is in the glaciers of the Arctic, the Antarctic, and mountains around the world. Water is considered a renewable resource. It is renewed through the water cycle.

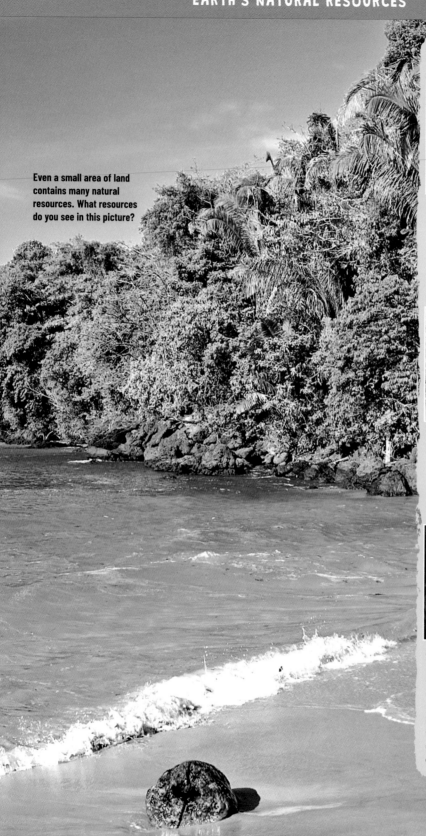

Even a small area of land contains many natural resources. What resources do you see in this picture?

A WEALTH OF RESOURCES

Soil

Rich soil is a resource farmers work hard to protect. Many of today's farmers have learned ways to fight erosion and keep the soil healthy – while still getting a good crop.

Diamonds

Diamonds are a type of mineral. Like other minerals, they occur naturally. People value diamonds and other gemstones because they are so beautiful and difficult to find.

Almost Anything Imaginable

Everything these moviegoers are enjoying comes from natural resources. The fabric and metal in the seats come from cotton and iron ore. The popcorn comes from fields of corn. Even the electricity used to power the projector comes from natural resources.

Defining Natural Resources

Natural resources may be grouped in several ways. One way is to list them as either renewable or nonrenewable. Renewable resources are those that nature can replace, recycle, or regrow in a short time. Animals, plants, water, solar (sun) energy, and wind energy are examples of renewable resources. But remember: even renewable resources can be used up if we waste them.

Other resources are nonrenewable. This means that nature needs millions of years to create them. Examples of nonrenewable resources include oil, coal, natural gas, gold, silver, platinum, and other minerals. Today, people are using up these resources more quickly than nature can replenish them. When our supply of nonrenewable resources runs out, there won't be more.

Fish from oceans, rivers, and lakes are renewable resources. However, overfishing is threatening the survival of some types of fish, such as the tuna that have been caught in this picture.

Most trees are said to be renewable, but replacing an old redwood tree - known as old growth - can take hundreds of years. So, old-growth trees are called nonrenewable.

LOSING RESOURCES

The Quagga: Extinct

Thousands of quagga once grazed on the plains of southern Africa, but they were hunted to extinction in the wild in about 1870. The last quagga in captivity died in a zoo in Amsterdam in 1883.

Hawaiian Birds: Threatened

The mongoose was brought to Hawaii in 1883 to help control the islands' rat population and protect their crops. However, mongooses began eating bird eggs, thereby threatening Hawaii's ground-nesting birds.

Before   After

The Aral Sea: Lost

The Aral Sea sat on the border between Khazakstan and Uzbekistan. Since it started to be used for irrigation in the 1960s, it has be shrinking. It has now almost completely disappeared, leaving behind a desert.

What Kind of Resource is Soil?

Some natural resources are not easy to list as either renewable or nonrenewable. Soil is one example. Although many people consider soil nonrenewable, it can be renewed. But it takes many, many years. Nature may need thousands of years to make just an inch of healthy, mineral-rich soil.

Iron ore is an inorganic resource. Here it is heated to create steel in a process called smelting. The large, hot, orange, steel sheet is being rolled by a machine in a steel mill.

Organic Resources

Natural resources can also be grouped as either organic or inorganic. Organic resources come from things that are, or were, once alive. These include plants and animals. Think about all of the ways to use organic resources in a day. You might wear clothes made out of cotton or lamb's wool. Lunch might be a cheese sandwich and an apple. Your school work is written on paper, maybe at a desk - both of which are made out of wood.

Inorganic Resources

Other natural resources are inorganic. Inorganic resources do not come from living organisms. Minerals and rocks are examples of inorganic materials. Our daily lives are filled with examples of these resources, too. The soda can you recycled today is made from aluminum. Your mother's earrings might have opals in them. The construction crew down the street is using steel in the buildings being put up.

As a renewable organic resource, trees are often grown in order to be harvested, just like many other plants. Whole forests may be grown (above left) specifically to be cut down for the wood they produce. Meanwhile the careful cultivating of new crops of trees (above right) assures that these resources stay renewable.

Wool: An Organic Resource

Wool is only one product that sheep provide us with. We also eat their meat (as lamb or mutton) and make cheeses (such as feta cheese) and yogurt from their milk.

Sheep produce a fleece.

The sheep is sheared.

The fleece is spun into yarn.

Yarn is made into clothes and other textiles.

ORGANIC OR INORGANIC?

Examine the following list and decide whether each item listed comes from an organic or inorganic resource. (answers are at the bottom of the page)

1) Drinking glass
2) Honey
3) Icicle
4) Cooking oil made from corn or sunflowers
5) Leather ball
6) Cell phone
7) Spaghetti sauce
8) Baseball bat

Look around the room. Add items that you can see to your list. Do they come from organic or inorganic resources?

In simple terms, organic means anything that comes from a plant or an animal. Inorganic describes anything that was never living.

ANSWERS: 1. Inorganic 2. Organic 3. Inorganic 4. Organic 5. Organic 6. Inorganic 7. Organic 8. Organic

Natural gas forms along with oil. Early oil drillers considered it worthless. They burned it just to get rid of it! Some countries do that even today.

2. NONRENEWABLE RESOURCES

Nonrenewable resources are found on Earth in limited amounts. This means that they cannot be replaced easily. At least, that is, they cannot be replaced as quickly as many of them are being used. And people have been using some of them at an increasing rate for years.

Fossil Fuels

Many nonrenewable resources are fossil fuels. Among these are oil, natural gas, and coal. They are called fossil fuels because they were made from the decaying remains of animals, plants, and other organisms.

These materials have been forming in Earth's crust (the outermost solid layer of the Earth) for millions of years. Some of this matter fell to the ocean floor and was covered over by sediment. Some of the matter was buried deep in the ground. In either case, the decay was covered over by layer after layer of other materials. It all became part of Earth's crust. There it sat for millions of years, compressed beneath the heat and weight of the matter covering it. Slowly the material formed fossil fuels.

Drilling for Oil

The first oil well was drilled in Titusville, Pennsylvania, USA, in 1859. There, a retired railroad conductor named Edwin Drake struck oil on his farm. People were first interested in oil for use in kerosene lamps. Use for cars and heating came later, but Drake's discovery was the beginning of the modern oil industry. His well was the first drilled just for the purpose of finding oil.

FOSSIL FUELS: WORLD CONSUMPTION 1965–2019

- Other renewables
- Biofuels
- Solar
- Wind
- Hydropower
- Nuclear
- Gas
- Coal
- Oil

This chart shows how the consumption of fossil fuels (coal, gas, and oil) has increased dramatically between the 1965 and 2019. Note also the gradual rise in alternative, renewable energy sources, such as solar, wind and hydropower.

These rigs drill for oil around the clock. We use this oil in our cars and to heat our homes. The oil was formed from organisms that lived in water millions of years ago. Oil deposits found today might once have been covered by oceans or seas.

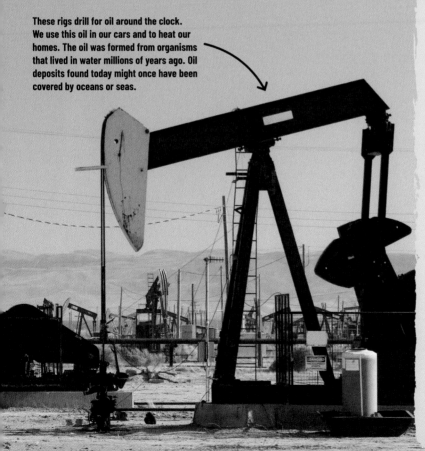

HOW COAL IS FORMED

PEAT

300 MILLION YEARS AGO - SWAMP

About 300 million years ago, tree-filled swamps covered much of the Earth. As plants and trees died, they settled to the bottom of these swamps. There, this matter began to decay.

SEDIMENT

LIGNITE

Heat and Pressure

100 MILLION YEARS AGO - OCEAN

The decaying matter formed peat. This spongy material was soon buried under more layers.

SEDIMENT

Heat and Pressure

COAL

TODAY

After millions of years of pressure and heat, the peat became coal.

Using Fossil Fuels

Currently, over 80 percent of the energy used worldwide comes from fossil fuels. Most of these fossil fuels, such as oil, natural gas, and coal, must be changed, or converted in some way, to create energy that we can reuse. Today, through technology, we are able to convert fossil fuels to usable energy more and more efficiently.

Oil and natural gas are very much in demand as energy sources today. And no wonder! They power our vehicles, they heat our homes and businesses and they are also used to make plastics, medicines, cosmetics, synthetic fabrics, and many other products.

Oil is used in the production of items we might not ever imagine it to be used for, such as ink for printing money, asphalt for roads, lipstick, and even trainers.

A LOOK AT HOW FOSSIL FUELS ARE USED (BY RANK)

FOSSIL FUEL	MAJOR PRODUCERS	USE OF FOSSIL FUEL
Oil	USA, Saudi Arabia, Russia	• As petrol, diesel fuel, jet fuel to power cars, buses, trains, and planes • Heating oil • In the manufacturing of plastics, synthetic clothing (such as nylon, polyester, kevlar), cosmetics, medicines, fertilizers, insecticides, etc.
Coal	China, India, USA	• Fuel for heat, light, and generating electricity
Natural Gas	Russia, Iran, Qatar	• Fuel for lighting, heating, cooking, manufacturing, and generating electricity

La Brea: Treasure Trove of Death

Tar pits form when crude oil from Earth's crust seeps up to the surface through cracks in the crust. The La Brea Tar Pits in Los Angeles, USA, are famous for their collection of fossilized animals and plants from the Pleistocene Period. The remains of insects, reptiles, amphibians, birds, fish, and even mammals, such as saber-toothed tigers (as above), have been discovered.

Population and Consumption

Three countries - China, USA and India - consume more fossil fuels than the rest of the world combined! There are various reasons for this, one of which is population. 43 percent of people in the world live in one of these three countries. China has the largest population of any country and has the highest fossil fuel consumption, but per person, they only consume half as much as the USA. In turn, the USA consumes less per person than some much smaller countries.

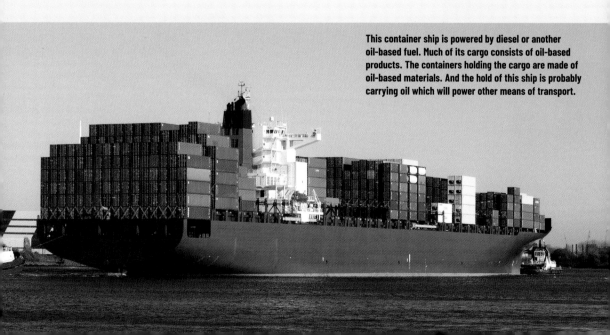

This container ship is powered by diesel or another oil-based fuel. Much of its cargo consists of oil-based products. The containers holding the cargo are made of oil-based materials. And the hold of this ship is probably carrying oil which will power other means of transport.

Problems with Fossil Fuels

Humans have found many uses for coal, natural gas, and oil, but using these fossil fuels also has its problems; the biggest of which is pollution. Most fossil fuels must be burned to be used. Burning them releases their energy. Only then do they create heat, produce electricity, or otherwise perform as we need them to. As they burn, however, they also release harmful pollutants into the atmosphere, including:

- **Carbon dioxide:** Plants and trees rely on this gas to survive, but too much of it in our atmosphere leads to global warming.

- **Carbon monoxide:** This adds to urban smog, air pollution, and global warming.

- **Sulphur dioxide:** This comes from coal and causes acid rain.

- **Release particulates:** These small bits of matter are released by burning fuel and are not healthy for people to breathe.

We call this release of substances *emissions*.

In large urban settings such as Los Angeles (right), burning fossil fuels causes air pollution. Exhaust from cars, trucks, and other vehicles is a major contributor.

GLOBAL EMISSIONS OF CARBON DIOXIDE (CO$_2$)

CARBON DIOXIDE EMISSIONS IN METRIC TONNES

35 Billion
30 Billion
25 Billion
20 Billion
15 Billion
10 Billion
5 Billion

1965 1970 1980 1990 2000 2010 2018

This chart shows the rise in global emissions of carbon dioxide from burning fossil fuels, from 1965 to 2018. In the last 10 years growth in emissions has started to slow, but it is still on the rise.

Underground mines put miners in danger of mine collapse and lung disease from breathing coal dust. But strip mining (above) can scar the land as the topsoil is stripped away to get at the coal beneath.

A Risky Business

Fossil fuels are often buried deep in the earth - right where they formed. They are brought to the surface by mining, drilling, piping, or other means. These methods can be harmful to both the planet and the people who collect them.

Oil Spills

Oil spills are a danger whenever crude oil must be transported. Spills can kill animals and destroy whole ecosystems. They can also harm communities and industries along the coasts. In 1979, the tanker Atlantic Empress, collided with the tanker, Aegean Captain. The two ships spilled over 304,000 tons (276,000 metric tonnes) of oil into the Caribbean Sea. This is the worst oil tanker spill on record.

Not Just for Jewelry

Many diamonds come from Africa, but Russia, Canada, Australia, and Brazil are also big suppliers of diamonds. Mining diamonds can be brutal, dangerous work. Diamonds are not only used in expensive jewelry. As the hardest known mineral, they are used in industry for grinding, polishing, and cutting machine parts and other hard substances – including other diamonds!

Mineral and Rock Resources

Minerals and rocks are also nonrenewable resources. They make up Earth's crust and other solid parts of our planet.

A Huge and Varied Resource

Scientists have identified 3,800 different minerals. Some, such as ores, contain metals. The metals can be stripped out and used in building and manufacturing. Metals are especially useful in electrical supplies as they are good conductors of heat and electricity. Other rare minerals, like rubies and emeralds, are used in jewelry. Precious metals like gold, silver, and platinum may also be used in jewelry and other luxury items.

A Stable and Reliable Resource

The term mineral is often used for anything nonliving taken from the ground. But it actually refers to specific substances. True minerals have

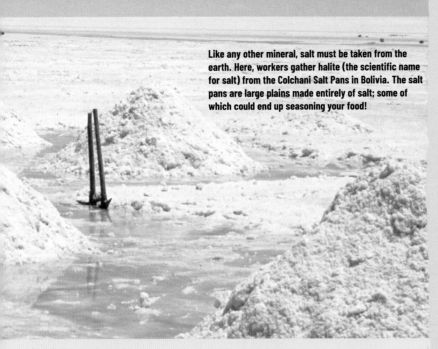

Like any other mineral, salt must be taken from the earth. Here, workers gather halite (the scientific name for salt) from the Colchani Salt Pans in Bolivia. The salt pans are large plains made entirely of salt; some of which could end up seasoning your food!

METALS: A USEFUL RESOURCE

Metals are often extracted from other resources, such as minerals. Once mined, a metal can be combined with other substances to produce an alloy.

Nickel

Nickel is used mostly as an alloy. Combined with iron, it gives great strength to steel. The nickel used in coins is actually an alloy made up mostly of copper.

set chemical makeups. A mineral will be the same no matter where it is found. This is not true of rocks. Samples of the same type of rock may have very different chemical makeups.

Tungsten

Tungsten melts at 6,170°F (3,410°C), making it the most heat-resistant metal known. It is used as the wire filament in traditional halogen light bulbs.

THE PROPERTIES OF MINERALS: A SHORT GLOSSARY

Some common properties of minerals include the following:

Color: a mineral's true color.

Hardness: this is measured on a scale of hardness devised by German geologist Friedrich Mohs.

Cleavage: the way a mineral breaks along its planes in parallel lines and creates a smooth surface. Mica is known for this.

Fracture: the way a mineral separates if it does not break along its planes.

Specific gravity: a mineral's weight compared to an equal volume of water.

Lustre: the way a mineral reflects light.

Crystal form: the arrangement of a mineral's atoms. Amethyst's crystal form shows in angular shapes on its surface.

COPPER

MICA

AMETHYST

Aluminum

Aluminum is lightweight yet strong. It can be shaped easily when heated and stays tough under extreme cold. Aluminium is one of the most useful metals known. It is used for foil, cans, and in building materials.

HELPING ECOSYSTEMS HELP THEMSELVES

By monitoring the condition of Earth's ecosystems, we can help nature maintain a balance among the many renewable resources that keep them healthy.

Cutting Down With Care

Forests can stay renewable as long as people help forests replenish their own supply of trees. Planned and controlled logging keeps forests free of sick or dying trees.

Managing Animal Numbers

Control of animal populations assures food for all. Too many fish in one place can choke off their food supply. Overfishing can deprive water resources of their balance between plant and animal life.

Water for All

Dams control the flow of water and create lakes and reservoirs. These provide a source of drinking water and recreation for humans, and drinking water and habitats for wildlife.

3. RENEWABLE RESOURCES

Earth's renewable resources are those that can be replaced in a short amount of time. Energy from the Sun, water, wind, animals and plants are all renewable resources.

Smart and Necessary

Even the air we breathe and heat produced inside the Earth are resources. Water, sunlight and plants are crucial to life on the planet. So taking care of Earth's renewable resources isn't just smart – it is necessary.

Ecosystems: Renewable Resources at Work

An ecosystem is a community in nature. It is any place where plants and animals depend on each other for food. Within that ecosystem the animals and plants are a renewable resource. The animals and plants also depend on other renewable resources, such as water and the Sun, to exist in their ecosystem.

In a garden, plants rely on the soil, and the atmosphere, for water and carbon dioxide. They also use energy from sunlight to convert the carbon dioxide and water into food (carbohydrates). Honeybees, birds, and other animals eat the plants or drink their nectar. In turn, these animals carry pollen from one plant to another. This helps the plants to reproduce.

Meat-eating animals eat plant-eating animals. The nutrition produced by plants then enters the meat-eaters' bodies.

SOLAR-POWERED SUN TEA

Materials needed
- A large clear jug/container (with cover)
- Cold water
- 2-6 tea bags, depending on the size of the container
- Glasses, lots of ice, lemon, and sugar or an artificial sweetener

1) Fill your container with water. Add the tea bags. Place the container in a sunny place. Allow tea to brew in the sunlight. This may take several hours.

2) When the tea has brewed to a dark color, remove the tea bags. Be sure to refrigerate your Sun tea as soon as it's brewed. Cool your tea in the refrigerator, or add plenty of ice, lemon, or sugar or sweetener and drink immediately. Enjoy your solar-powered iced tea!

! The Sun's energy is there for the taking. Test that idea by making yourself some Sun tea. Even a slightly gray day will give you enough power from the Sun to provide the energy needed for water to heat up and brew a large container of tea.

Water. Air. Wind. Sun. We live every day with a number of renewable resources at our fingertips. Earth has more renewable than nonrenewable resources.

Alternative Energy Sources

Whether it be solar energy, wind energy, hydroelectric power, biomass, geothermal power or tidal power, people are increasingly turning to alternative means of energy production to reduce, or replace, the use of fossil fuels.

While fossil fuels will run out one day, renewable energy sources will always be available. Most of them are also far more environmentally friendly, causing little to no air pollution and contributing much less to global warming. However, we currently still rely far more on nonrenewable energy sources. Renewables made up 26.2 percent of global electricity generation in 2018. That's expected to rise to 45 percent by 2040.

Heated water from the Svartsengi Geothermal Power Plant in Grindavik, Iceland, flows to a famous health spa called Blue Lagoon.

Geothermal Power

Geothermal power comes from using the heat of the Earth itself. This heat, in the form of hot water and steam, is often found in areas of volcanic activity. With pipes and pumps, the water or steam is taken from underground reservoirs. It is used to power turbines that then generate electricity.

Wind Power

Wind power is created by harnessing the power of the wind. In the past, people used windmills. Today they use powerful wind turbines. Both capture the energy from the wind, using it to turn the blades at the top of a tower. Today, a wind turbine's turning blades are used to generate electricity.

Despite the benefits of wind power, some people think a hillside dotted with giant wind turbines, as seen here in the Mojave Desert in the US, is an eyesore and makes too much noise.

Tidal Power

Like hydroelectric power, tidal power also uses energy from water. In this case, the energy is generated by the tides that advance and recede in the oceans and large lakes. Dams stretching over bays capture water at high tide. Later, as water is released with the outgoing tide, the movement powers turbines and generates electricity. There is some evidence that this method can have a negative impact on wildlife.

This is the first tidal power station, which was build on the Rance River's estuary in Brittany, France.

ALTERNATE ENERGIES AT WORK

Solar Power

Solar power comes from the Sun. Energy from the Sun is collected by capturing its rays in special solar panels. This energy is converted to electricity, which can be used for many different purposes. In the picture above, a parking meter is powered by a solar panel.

Hydroelectric Power

Hydroelectric power is generated by moving water. Power plants built over flowing rivers convert the water's energy into electrical energy. First the water is stored behind a dam. As the water is released, the movement turns huge turbine blades. This, in turn generates electricity.

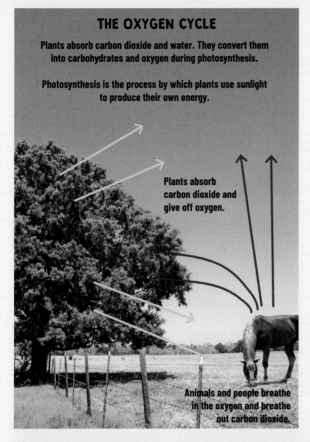

THE OXYGEN CYCLE

Plants absorb carbon dioxide and water. They convert them into carbohydrates and oxygen during photosynthesis.

Photosynthesis is the process by which plants use sunlight to produce their own energy.

Plants absorb carbon dioxide and give off oxygen.

Animals and people breathe in the oxygen and breathe out carbon dioxide.

Plant Resources

It would be easy to overlook plants as valuable natural resources. They are so much a part of our lives. As part of the oxygen cycle, plants play a key role in renewing the oxygen in Earth's atmosphere. Without plants, humans and animals would not have oxygen to breathe.

Plants are also a food resource in all of Earth's ecosystems. For humans in particular, plants are a food source whether growing wild or as crops that we plant and harvest.

Rainforest Treasure

Many scientists think that about two-thirds of all plant species in the world are found in rainforests. These plants produce as much as 40 percent of Earth's oxygen. Rainforest plants have given us hundreds of varieties of fruits, vegetables, spices,

Warm, wet rainforests—like this one in Madagascar—have more kinds of trees than anywhere else on Earth. Protecting rainforests also means protecting countless plant and animal species.

and coffee. The raw materials for many products, from chewing gum to rubber, come from rainforest trees.

Medicine Cabinet to the World

Scientists estimate that plants from the rainforest have provided the basis for about 25 percent of the world's medicines. From compounds that help heal wounds to drugs that fight cancer, especially leukemia and other childhood cancers: Earth's rainforests could hold the promise for future success in treating illness and disease.

Cutting Carbon

Rainforests are very good at storing and absorbing large quantities of carbon dioxide from the atmosphere, because of the many trees and plants that they contain. The more forests that are destroyed, the fewer trees there are to perform this important job. This leads to a rise in global warming.

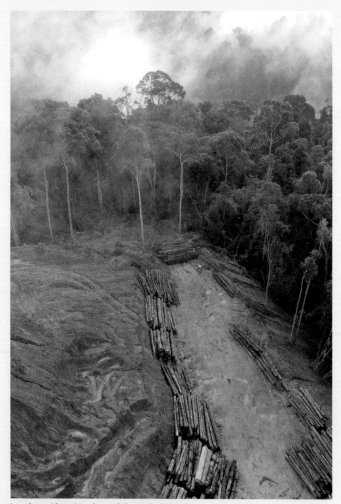

Logging taking place in a rainforest in Malaysia.

Paper or Forests?

It's no secret that Earth's rainforests are in danger. Around 8 million hectares (31,000 square miles) of rainforest are cut down. That's an area the size of South Carolina in the USA, or the whole of the Czech Republic! Most of the logging industry is based on the demand for wood and paper products. About 95 percent of all paper is made from wood, but now paper can be efficiently and successfully reused through recycling. Think of how much rainforest could be saved just from recycling the daily newspaper!*

* See the newspaper recycling experiment on page 29.

ANIMALS AT WORK

Pack Animals

Some animals have many uses. Llamas, like camels, horses, and even elephants, are called pack animals. This means they are used to carry things. Llamas also have hair that makes useful fiber for textiles.

Aquaculture

Some fish, such as salmon and trout, are both caught in the wild and farmed. Fish farming is known as aquaculture. As world supplies in the wild have declined, fish farming has grown. According to recent figures, over 40 percent of all fish eaten come from farms.

Whose Resource?

The North American Northern Spotted Owl prefers nesting in old-growth forests. Old-growth forests have lots of undergrowth and decaying trees. The owl has become the focus of a debate between environmental groups and companies that log these forests for their ancient and highly valuable trees.

Animal Resources

Just like plants, animals are a renewable resource. In thinking about animals as a resource, you might first think of them as sources of food or other products for people. Fish, for example, feed people all over the world. Sheep, goats, and cattle give milk and meat. Hides from many animals have value when building shelters or as clothing and shoes.

Animals also have a major effect on the environment. Each animal helps balance the ecosystem it is part of. Small fish feed people. They also feed sharks in the ocean. Coyotes have been known to kill sheep and sometimes get into rubbish in urban areas, but they also control the rodent population around farms and towns. Each of these animals plays an important role in its own ecosystem.

The Big Picture

Each individual ecosystem contributes to the health of our planet, which is a collection of ecosystems. Sometimes, however, humans exploit the resources in one ecosystem. We cut down too many trees in a rainforest or damage the landscape while mining for coal, or farming excessively. We have to think about the effect this might have on the planet as a whole.

Some animals, such as cattle, are such important resources that humans have domesticated, or tamed, them. Herds of cattle are kept all over the world.

GO WILD WHERE YOU LIVE!

Exploring the wildlife where you live gives you a chance to see nature up close, and may lead to some surprise discoveries! Try the following activities to learn more about the wildlife and natural resources near your home.

1) Using online sources, the library, or visits to a local zoo or nature center, find out what kinds of wildlife live in your area.

2) Be an observer of life around you! Keep track of the kinds of animal life you actually see near where you live. Write down what you observe in a notebook for one week.

3) Also observe what resources in your local area these animals rely on to survive. Are the resources organic or inorganic? Are they natural or made by humans?

4) Can you identify some ways in which the animals' resources might be threatened? For example, are homes or industrial buildings being built on wild areas that are an animal's habitat? Is a river in your area becoming polluted with trash?

The American Bison

In the 1800s, bison populations on the Great Plains of North America may have been as great as 30 to 75 million. Native Americans relied on the bison for food, clothing, and fuel. Non-Native settlers hunted the bison aggressively, nearly driving them to extinction. By the 1880s, the bison population may have been as low as 1,000. The government and conservationists worked to protect the bison, and its population has grown again. But it will never reach the huge numbers it once had.

WATER USE IN THE HOME

Here are some common uses of water in the home. Also shown is the average amount of water each activity uses.

- One bath: 21 gallons (80 liters)
- One shower: 9 gallons (35 liters)
- One toilet flush: 2 gallons (8 liters)
- One dishwasher load: 6.5 gallons (25 liters)
- One washing machine load: 17 gallons (65 liters)

In an average home which activity do you think uses the most water per day?

Answer: flushing the toilet

4. CONSERVATION: WHAT CAN YOU DO?

Taking care of our natural resources will help ensure that future generations have what they need to survive on our planet. It will also teach us to become responsible caretakers of the world we call home.

Reduce

You may have heard the expression 'Reduce, Reuse, Recycle.' Those who are concerned about the future of our planet feel that we must become better at reducing our need for natural resources.

Cutting back on the use of oil for transport will help conserve fossil fuels and also reduce the release of pollutants into the atmosphere.

The more we know about our interaction with Earth and its natural resources, the better off we will be.

In recent years technological advancements and increased enviromental awareness have led to an rise in the use of electric powered cars and public transport. In the next couple decades, petrol and diesel cars will become a thing of the past!

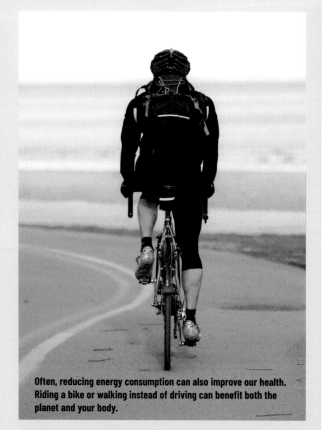

Often, reducing energy consumption can also improve our health. Riding a bike or walking instead of driving can benefit both the planet and your body.

HOW MUCH DO YOU USE?

 Try this experiment to figure out how much water you might use washing your hands in a year.

Materials needed:
- Large bowl
- Container with measuring markers

1) Wash your hands as normal, but place a large bowl in your sink to catch the water you use. Pour the used water into a measuring cup. How much have you used? Record the amount in a notebook.

2) Keep track of how many times you wash your hands in a day. Multiply the amount of water you used in your first hand washing by the number of times a day you washed.

3) Multiply the amount of water you use in one day by 365. This number should show roughly how much water you use just washing your hands in a year.

Did that total surprise you?

TAKING IT EASY WITH ENERGY

Planning for the Future

Some energy-saving solutions, like putting solar panels on a home, are more expensive to start with, but in the long run they will reduce our need for fossil fuels to provide homes and businesses with heat and other energy.

Every Little Counts

Your local electricity or water company offers many good ideas for conserving energy. Your family can install low-flowing showerheads and toilets. You can turn down the thermostat in the winter – and wear a jumper!

EARTHWORM COMPOSTERS

Some people use earthworm boxes as a way to compost. These boxes are made of wood or plastic and filled with shredded newspaper or cardboard and decaying leaves. A handful of soil should also be added. Soil is gritty and helps worms break down food particles. Boxes can be made at home or bought from garden supply stores.

In the box, the earthworms are fed kitchen scraps such as fruit and vegetable peelings, bread and egg shells. (Do not add meat scraps.) The worms eat this matter, which otherwise goes into landfills. Under ideal conditions each earthworm eats its own weight in waste every 24 hours.

The worms' droppings mix with the dirt in the box to make rich, nutrient-filled compost that can be used in the garden to feed plants or even to grow more vegetables!

Reuse

In addition to reducing our need for resources, reusing and recycling are two ways we can all play a role in conserving energy. Reusing allows us to make a second (or third or fourth) use of an existing object. Think about that box that brought a package to your door. Or the shopping bag you carried into the kitchen. Most items that we use to carry or send things in can be reused over and over.

Recycle

Recycling allows us to make new things out of used materials. Many materials can be recycled, such as paper, plastic, metal, and glass. Many of these materials are already part of recycling programs.

Most communities have recycling programs that allow us all to easily dispose of metal cans, drinks bottles, and newspapers. These programs give us a chance to enjoy the good feeling we all get when we know we have helped conserve our planet's resources.

This is paper collected from recycling points waiting to be processed and recycled.

Recycling products from home is one of the easiest ways to get involved in conservation efforts. Anyone can recycle!

MAKE RECYCLED PAPER

The newspapers and scrap paper you take to the recycling center is turned into pulp and then into new recycled paper. You can try making your own recycled paper at home or in your classroom.

Materials needed

- Large square or rectangular baking sheet
- A wash basin or mixing bowl
- 3 cups of water
- A newspaper
- A rolling pin

1) Tear one to two pages of newspaper into small pieces of 1 inch (2.5 cm) or less.

2) Put some of the paper pieces into a large bowl and add all the water. Keep adding paper. Tear and squeeze the paper until you get a mush that looks like thick porridge.

3) Turn the baking sheet upside down and put about 1 cup of the paper pulp over the bottom of the baking sheet. Spread the pulp evenly over the baking sheet with your fingers.

4) Lay several sheets of newspaper over the pulp to hold it onto the baking sheet. Carefully turn the baking sheet over and remove the sheet, so that your pulp layer is now sitting on the newspaper.

5) Fold the newspaper over the pulp. Roll the rolling pin over the newspaper parcel to blot out the extra water.

6) Uncover the pulp and let the sheet of new 'paper' dry completely!

GLOSSARY

acid rain Air pollution mixed with water in the atmosphere that then falls to Earth as rain. Acid rain contains pollution in the form of acids. It can dirty the soil and water, harm plants, and even damage hard surfaces such as stone.

alloy A substance made by combining metal with another material.

atmosphere The thick layer of air that surrounds the Earth. The gases that make up the Earth's atmosphere include nitrogen (78%) and oxygen (21%). There is also water, and small quantities of other gases such as argon and carbon dioxide.

atom All materials and subtances are made up of atoms. They are the smallest possible unit of an element that still behaves like that element.

carbon monoxide A poisonous gas formed in the burning of fossil fuels.

conservation This word means the 'planned management of natural resources'. In our everyday lives it means only using what we need. For example, we can conserve water by not leaving the tap running when we brush our teeth.

conservationist A person who works to protect Earth's natural resources. A conservationist may work to save rainforests and stop them being cut down.

crude oil The natural state of petroleum. This fossil fuel formed from decaying plants, animals, and other organisms. As crude oil comes from the ground, it is piped or shipped to a refinery. There, the crude oil is refined. It is used to produce a number of different fuels, including natural gas, petrol, kerosene, and more.

economy A system of exchange of goods and services.

ecosystem An ecosystem is a community in which animals and plants rely on each other and on resources such as water and sunlight. An ecosystem can be large like a woodland, or small, like a single tree.

element A substance made up of only one type of atom. Elements cannot be broken down into other substances.

erosion When land or rocks are worn away by the force of wind or rain.

extinct When an animal or plant no longer exists on Earth.

fossils Remains or imprints of ancient plants and animals that have been preserved in rocks.

fresh water Water sources, such as most rivers and lakes, that do not contain salt.

gemstones Precious rocks and minerals, such as rubies, emeralds, and pearls. They are often used in jewelry.

generation The lifespan of a group of living things, such as plants or animals. A generation is usually counted as being the period of time between the birth of a parent and the birth of their young.

geothermal power Energy, such as electricity, that is created by harnessing heat from within the Earth. Hot magma under the Earth's crust heats up water on the surface. Steam from the hot water is used to drive turbines in power stations.

global warming A gradual warming of the Earth's atmosphere. Most scientists believe that this is caused by humans burning fossils fuels, such as oil and coal. The burning of these fuels gives off gases that trap too much of the Sun's heat in the Earth's atmosphere.

habitat An environment in which a particular plant or animal does best and is most likely found.

hydroelectric power Electricity produced by power plants that use the energy created by moving water.

inorganic Something that is not living, such as metal or rock.

irrigation The process of bringing water to a place. For example pumping water from a river to irrigate (water) crops.

kerosene A thin, light oil used in lamps and heaters and for cleaning.

minerals Solid, usually inorganic, substances that occur naturally on Earth, such as gold, copper, iron and salt.

natural resources The materials, energy sources and living things found in nature that are useful to people and other living creatures. Water, air, minerals, the Sun's energy, plants and animals are all natural resources.

nitrogen oxides Gases produced in the burning of fossil fuels. Nitrogen oxides are one of the gases that contribute to acid rain.

nonrenewable Unable to be renewed. Fossil fuels and minerals, such as gemstones, are part of this group.

nuclear energy Energy stored in the nucleus, or core, of the atom. This energy is harnessed by releasing it from the atom. It can then be used to make electricity.

ore A rock or mineral containing metal that can be extracted (removed). Ores are mined for the metals they contain.

organic Something that is living, such as an animal or plant.

organism A living being.

overfishing Catching too many of a specific type of fish so that the population of that fish does not have time to breed and renew itself. Eventually overfishing of some fish species could lead to extinction.

particulates Small bits of substances, such as dirt and aerosol droplets, and other pollutants.

peat A brown material made from decayed plants, which is found in marshy places.

petroleum The substance, created by decaying plant and animal remains, from which oil, gas, and other products come.

politics A system of policies and practices influencing actions of a group of people.

pollinate To transfer pollen from one plant to another, in preparation for plant reproduction.

recede To move back.

renewable Able to be renewed. Plants and animals are renewable resources.

salt water Water, such as ocean water, that contains dissolved salts.

sediments Tiny grains of materials, such as rock and sand.

smog A foglike haze caused by pollution in the air. The word is formed by combining the words smoke and fog.

solar power Power created by harnessing the energy of the Sun as it reaches Earth.

sulphur oxide A gas that comes from the burning of fossil fuels and from natural occurrences such as volcanoes. It can be a major contributor to pollution.

tidal power Energy harnessed from the natural movement of bodies of water, such as oceans and lakes. Tidal power gets its energy from the natural rise and fall of the water at different times of the day.

volatile organics Chemicals, in the form of gases, that are released by products such as paint, glues and pesticides. They can cause pollution.

water cycle The constant movement of water from rivers, lakes, and the ocean up into the atmosphere and back down to Earth.

wind power Capturing the energy of the wind and using it to power windmills. The windmills drive turbines which produce electrical energy.

INDEX